# Inside Animals
# Penguins
## and Other Birds

David West

WINDMILL
BOOKS

Published in 2018 by **Windmill Books**,
an imprint of Rosen Publishing
29 East 21st Street, New York, NY 10010

Designed and illustrated *by* David West

CATALOGING-IN-PUBLICATION DATA
Names: West, David.
Title: Penguins and other birds / David West.
Description: New York : Windmill Books, 2018. | Series: Inside animals | Includes index.
Identifiers: ISBN 9781508194286 (pbk.) | ISBN 9781508193883 (library bound) |
ISBN 9781508194347 (6 pack))
Subjects: LCSH: Penguins–Juvenile literature. | Birds–Juvenile literature.
Classification: LCC QL697.W47 2018 | DDC 598–dc23

Manufactured in China
CPSIA Compliance Information: Batch BW18WM: For Further Information contact Rosen Publishing, New York, New York at 1-800-237-9932

# Contents

Penguin . . . . . . . . . . . . . . . . . . . . 4

Inside a Penguin . . . . . . . . . . . . . . 6

Chicken . . . . . . . . . . . . . . . . . . . 8

Inside a Chicken . . . . . . . . . . . . 10

Owl. . . . . . . . . . . . . . . . . . . . . . 13

Inside an Owl . . . . . . . . . . . . . . 14

Parrot. . . . . . . . . . . . . . . . . . . . 16

Inside a Parrot. . . . . . . . . . . . . . 18

Ostrich. . . . . . . . . . . . . . . . . . . 20

Inside an Ostrich . . . . . . . . . . . . 22

Glossary and Index. . . . . . . . . 24

# Penguin

Penguins are flightless birds that spend half of their time in the sea. Most can be found in the **southern hemisphere**. They use their wings like flippers to power their way through the water. They feed on fish and squid, catching them in their beaks underwater.

This king penguin dives to depths of more than 300 feet (91 m), and has been known to go as deep as 1,000 feet (304 m) when chasing its prey.

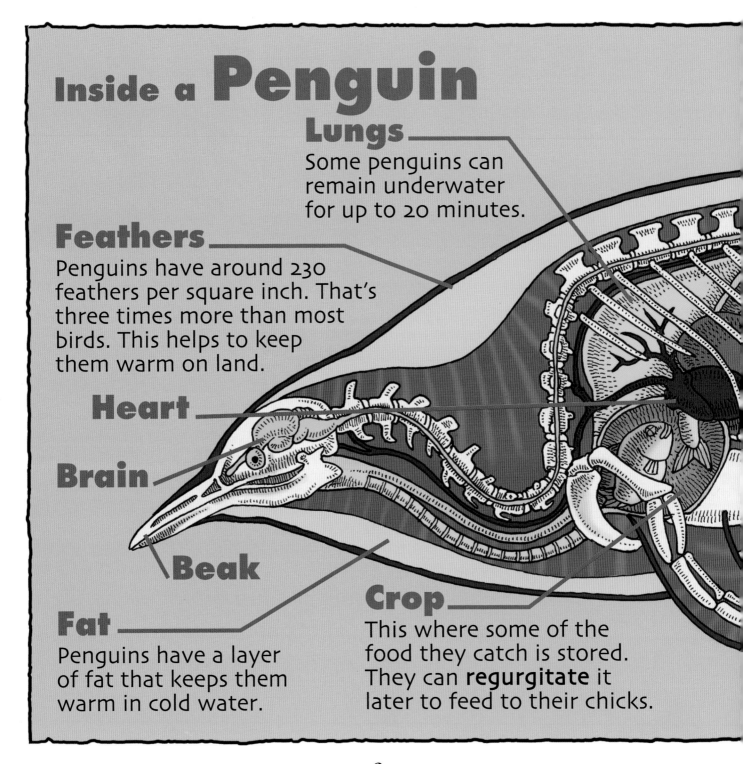

# Inside a **Penguin**

**Lungs**
Some penguins can remain underwater for up to 20 minutes.

**Feathers**
Penguins have around 230 feathers per square inch. That's three times more than most birds. This helps to keep them warm on land.

**Heart**

**Brain**

**Beak**

**Fat**
Penguins have a layer of fat that keeps them warm in cold water.

**Crop**
This where some of the food they catch is stored. They can **regurgitate** it later to feed to their chicks.

6

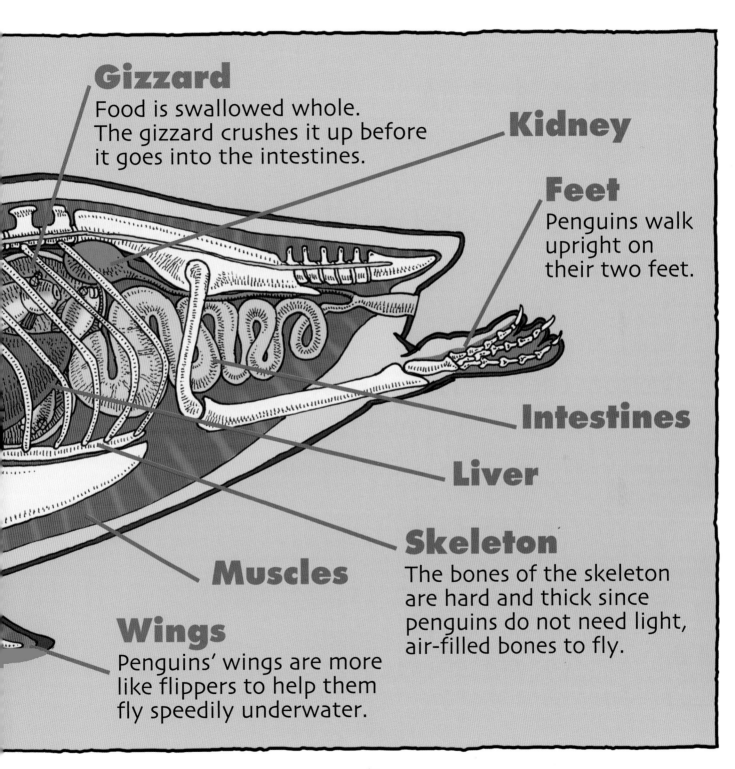

**Gizzard**
Food is swallowed whole.
The gizzard crushes it up before
it goes into the intestines.

**Kidney**

**Feet**
Penguins walk
upright on
their two feet.

**Intestines**

**Liver**

**Skeleton**
The bones of the skeleton
are hard and thick since
penguins do not need light,
air-filled bones to fly.

**Muscles**

**Wings**
Penguins' wings are more
like flippers to help them
fly speedily underwater.

# Chicken

Chickens are birds that are farmed for their eggs and as food. Females are called hens and males are called roosters. They eat seeds and insects, which they find by scratching the ground. In the wild, they may even eat small animals like lizards and mice. Chickens live together in flocks. They have a social order where some have first rights to food. This is known as a "pecking order."

*Chickens are descended from the red junglefowl and can fly a short distance. Usually, it is to **roost** in a tree or to escape a **predator**. Otherwise they don't bother.*

9

# Inside a **Chicken**

## Comb
Both roosters and hens have a comb and wattle. These fleshy parts of featherless skin are red.

## Brain
Tests have shown that chickens are more intelligent than people first realized.

## Wattle

## Feathers

## Crop
This is part of the chicken's digestive system where food is stored before it goes to its gizzard.

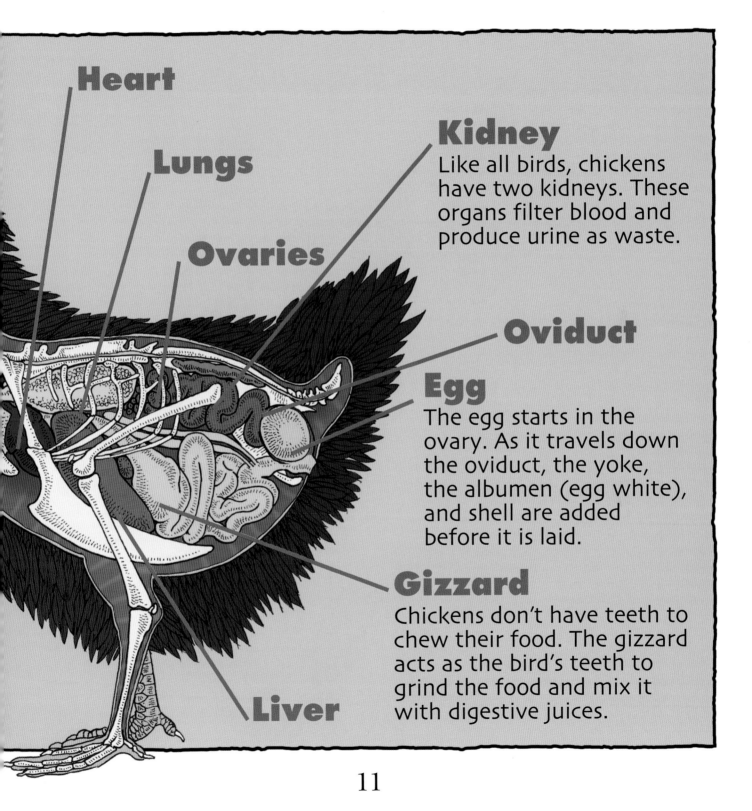

**Heart**

**Lungs**

**Ovaries**

**Kidney**
Like all birds, chickens have two kidneys. These organs filter blood and produce urine as waste.

**Oviduct**

**Egg**
The egg starts in the ovary. As it travels down the oviduct, the yoke, the albumen (egg white), and shell are added before it is laid.

**Gizzard**
Chickens don't have teeth to chew their food. The gizzard acts as the bird's teeth to grind the food and mix it with digestive juices.

**Liver**

# Owl

Owls are **birds of prey** that hunt at night. They have very good night vision and can rotate their heads and necks as much as 270°. They use their special ears to detect prey at night. They hunt insects, birds, and small mammals such as mice.

*Barn owls eat their prey whole, but they can't digest fur or bone. So they regurgitate these in the form of a pellet.*

# Inside an Owl

## Eyes

Barn owls' eyes are twice as good as human eyes in the dark. They are very good at seeing movement at night.

## Brain

## Face

Barn owls have a flat, disk-shaped face that collects and directs sound toward the ears.

## Beak

Like other birds of prey, barn owls have sharp, hooked beaks, which they use to tear up their food.

## Ears

Barn owls have the best hearing of all animals. They can capture prey in total darkness by hearing alone.

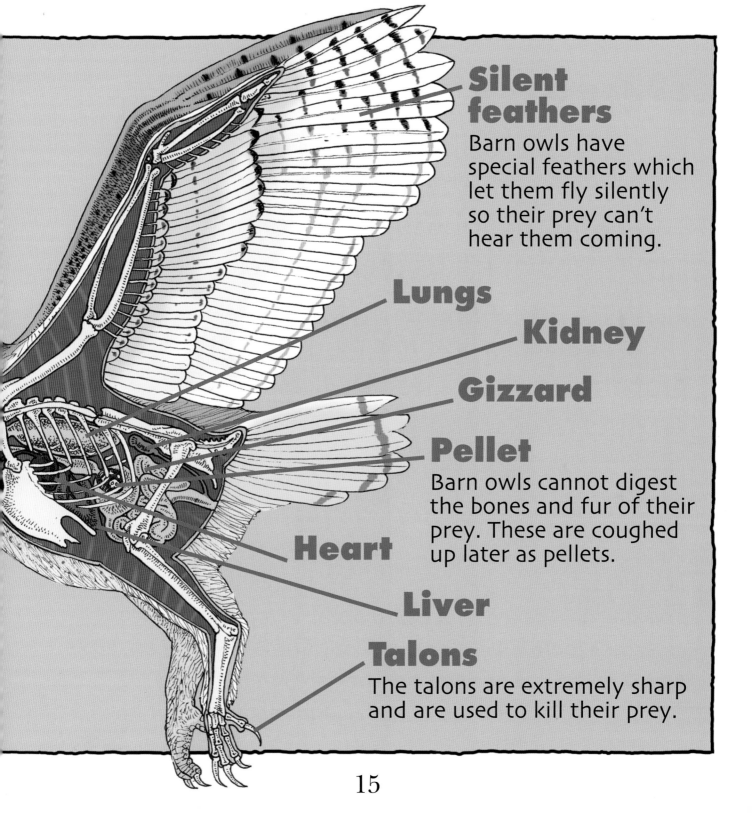

## Silent feathers

Barn owls have special feathers which let them fly silently so their prey can't hear them coming.

**Lungs**

**Kidney**

**Gizzard**

## Pellet

Barn owls cannot digest the bones and fur of their prey. These are coughed up later as pellets.

**Heart**

**Liver**

## Talons

The talons are extremely sharp and are used to kill their prey.

# Parrot

Parrots are intelligent birds that can **mimic** human speech. They are often kept as pets because of their beautiful colors. In the wild, they spend much of their time climbing around tree canopies. They also use their beak for climbing by gripping branches with it. They feed mainly on nuts, seeds, and fruits.

*This parrot is called a love bird because it pairs up with a partner for life. Pairs spend a lot of time perched on branches next to each other. They are among the smallest parrots and live in Africa and Madagascar.*

# Inside a **Parrot**

## Skeleton

A bird's skeleton is extremely light and strong. The bones are filled with holes.

## Brain

Parrots are intelligent. They have more brain cells than apes, despite having much smaller brains.

## Beak

Parrots use their sharp beaks to defend themselves. They also use them to crack nuts and peel fruits.

## Air sacs

Birds need to breathe lots of air to get enough oxygen for their muscles to fly. Lungs are backed up by up to eight air sacs around the body.

## Crop

## Keel

This breast bone is where the large flying muscles are attached.

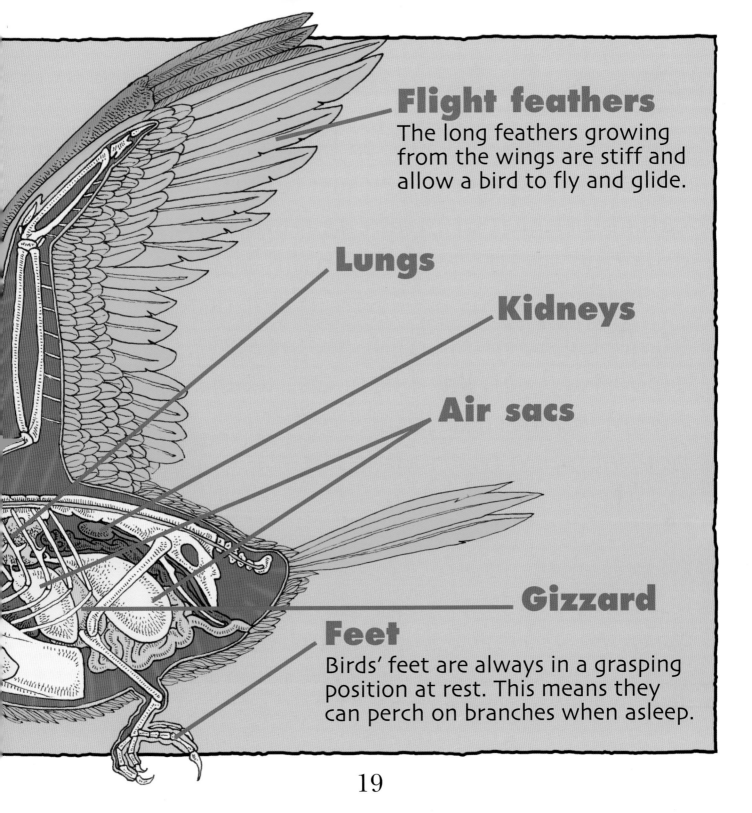

**Flight feathers**
The long feathers growing from the wings are stiff and allow a bird to fly and glide.

**Lungs**

**Kidneys**

**Air sacs**

**Gizzard**

**Feet**
Birds' feet are always in a grasping position at rest. This means they can perch on branches when asleep.

19

# Ostrich

The ostrich is a flightless bird. It is also the largest living bird. They are fast runners and can sprint at more than 43.5 mph (70 km/h), covering up to 16 feet (5 m) in a single stride. Their strong legs are used in self defense against predators. Their kick is so powerful it can kill a lion. Ostriches live in wandering groups of between five to 50 birds.

*When threatened, an ostrich will lie flat on the ground or run away. Sometimes it might kick out to defend itself. But it never hides its head in the sand.*

# Inside an Ostrich

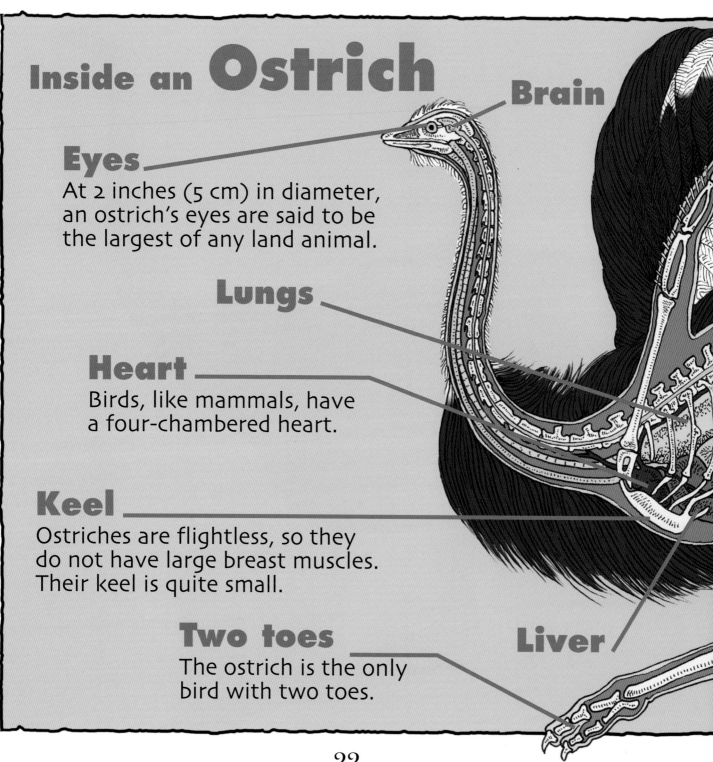

**Brain**

## Eyes

At 2 inches (5 cm) in diameter, an ostrich's eyes are said to be the largest of any land animal.

## Lungs

## Heart

Birds, like mammals, have a four-chambered heart.

## Keel

Ostriches are flightless, so they do not have large breast muscles. Their keel is quite small.

## Two toes

The ostrich is the only bird with two toes.

**Liver**

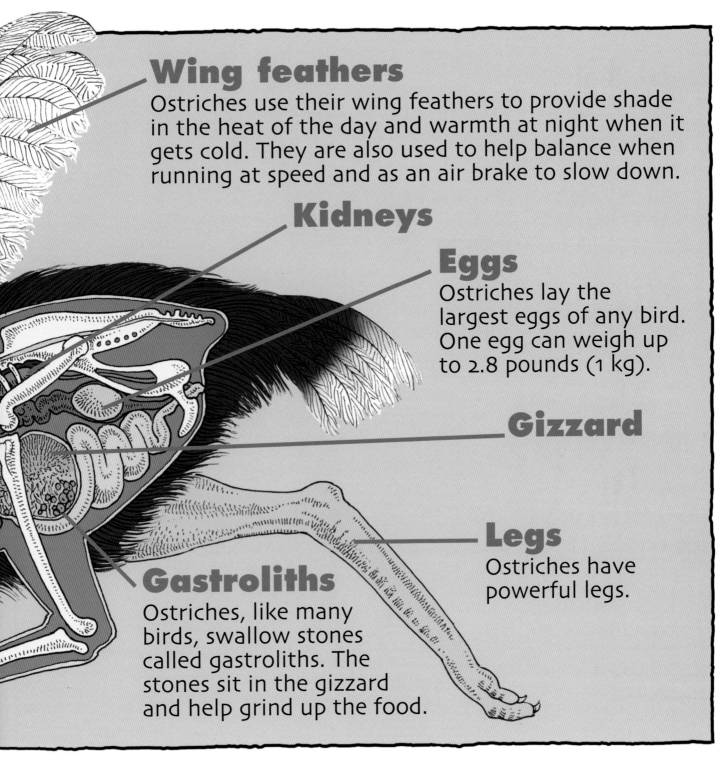

## Wing feathers

Ostriches use their wing feathers to provide shade in the heat of the day and warmth at night when it gets cold. They are also used to help balance when running at speed and as an air brake to slow down.

## Kidneys

## Eggs

Ostriches lay the largest eggs of any bird. One egg can weigh up to 2.8 pounds (1 kg).

## Gizzard

## Legs

Ostriches have powerful legs.

## Gastroliths

Ostriches, like many birds, swallow stones called gastroliths. The stones sit in the gizzard and help grind up the food.

# Glossary

**birds of prey** Also called raptors, these types of birds hunt birds, rodents, and other small animals. They have powerful talons and curved, sharp beaks.

**mimic** Copy or imitate.

**predator** An animal that hunts and eats other animals.

**regurgitate** Bring swallowed food back up to the mouth.

**roost** A perch, such as a branch, on which birds rest at night.

**southern hemisphere** The half of planet Earth which is south of the equator.

# Index

air sacs 18, 19

barn owl 13–15
beak 4, 6, 14, 16, 18, 24
birds of prey 13, 24

chicken 8, 10, 11
crop 6, 10, 18

feathers 6, 10, 15, 19, 23

gastroliths 23
gizzard 7, 10, 11, 15, 19, 23

junglefowl 8

king penguin 5

love bird 16

ostrich 20, 22, 23
owl 13–15

parrot 16, 18
penguin 4–7
predators 8, 20
prey 5, 13, 14, 15

wings 4, 7, 19